Developing Professional Skills: INCOME TAXATION

Stephanie Hunter McMahon
Professor of Law
University of Indiana
Maurer School of Law

Series Editor: Colleen Medill

WEST ACADEMIC

860 Blue Gentian Road, Suite 350
Eagan, MN 55121
1-877-888-1330

Published in the United States of America

ISBN: 979-8-89209-120-6

Preface

Professional legal skills require complex thinking about problems and the way lawyers use the law to solve those problems. Skills training thus focuses legal education on the end product of being an advisor to a specific client as opposed to seeing the law as an abstract tool. These skills are important and need to be taught throughout law school. The legal profession, most law school students, and many professors understand this.

Nevertheless, because skills training requires the application of doctrinal law to specific factual situations, it can be challenging to incorporate this training in a traditional course. Especially in a course as full of diverse and often complex topics as an introductory federal income tax course, doctrinal coverage already imposes time pressure. Despite the difficulty, situating abstract tax law into specific legal situations for which students provide legal advice helps students ground doctrinal law. It also helps them learn about the ways in which lawyers use this type of law.

In addition to reinforcing professional legal skills themselves, this book is also intended to introduce students to the diversity that exists within tax practice. For example, exercises include both tax controversy and tax planning work. These exercises provide an opening for an instructor to briefly explain topics that might otherwise be omitted from an introductory tax course, such as an overview of the audit and appeals process, applications for a private letter ruling or for 501(c)(3) status, or how tax fits within a standard term sheet in a business negotiation. The goal of these exercises is not to teach these subjects in their entirety but to introduce students to them and to the skills necessary for this type of work.

These exercises are not framed with the expectation that students intend to be tax specialists. Instead, they are problems involving tax issues that students in a wide variety of legal practices may experience.

Developing Professional Skills: Federal Income Tax is designed to provide skills training within this traditional course. Core skills developed are:

- Client counseling: engaging a new client, interviewing, gathering, and assembling facts
- Legal drafting: revising various transactional documents and client communications
- Negotiation and advocacy: negotiating issues with the rules and client in mind

Each chapter covers a core concept taught in a typical introductory federal income tax course in a problem involving client representation. Depending upon the teacher's prerogative, students are expected to spend about 1 to 2 hours preparing for the assignment in each chapter. Class time to discuss the material can take a minimum of 5 or 10 minutes per chapter for a focused debriefing on some aspect of the assignment.

There is an assumption in these exercises that students have access to and are learning the Internal Revenue Code and Treasury Regulations in the course's doctrinal discussions, but because of the diverse ways in which the course may be taught, simple descriptions of the law relevant to the particular issue are provided in each chapter. There are optional research questions to encourage students to practice their research skills and in the hope that students take an interest in the material and explore more broadly.

To facilitate ease of teaching, this book is accompanied by comprehensive Teachers Manual (TM). The TM provides a common template to analyze each problem. This template includes a discussion of the law, the relevant skill, the professional responsibility issues, and the norms of modern legal practice.

This book is not intended to fundamentally change the teaching method in a traditional doctrinal course. To balance the need to devote significant class time to the analysis of complex rules in a complex area of law, this book is intended to introduce skills-training primarily outside of class time. It uses the doctrinal course to reiterate the importance of teaching and learning skills. Of course, these problems cannot simulate all of the complexities in a modern legal practice. Nevertheless, using this book to focus on legal skills can enhance a student's education by helping them learn the legal practice associated with the federal income tax.

Introduction

Developing Professional Skills: Income Taxation introduces you to a variety of skills that differentiate a law student from an experienced tax practitioner. "Skills" include the set of competencies and professional tasks necessary to solve clients' legal problems. The competencies covered in this book are those needed by most first and second year attorneys in a variety of legal practices plus some of the material to be tested on the NextGen bar exam. These competencies include the abilities to: (1) interact professionally with clients to solicit important facts and circumstances; (2) evaluate facts and circumstances for relevance and to identify important legal issues; (3) formulate legal advice by weighing the facts and circumstances of the client's problem; and (4) produce various kinds of legal work product, including formal letters and transactional documents.

Like any type of skill, acquiring professional legal skills takes practice. Each chapter in this book provides you with an opportunity to practice a legal skill that you are likely to use shortly after graduation. The chapters of this book are organized according to topics that are usually covered in the introductory federal income tax course. Some foundational skills that one would expect to use frequently are covered in more than one chapter. The more the skills are practiced, the better they become. The following is the lesson plan:

Chapter 1, *Income: It's Great, Not Gross.* You meet with a prospective client who needs advice with respect to how she's been compensating her employees.

Chapter 2, *Loans: Forgiveness Is Tax-Free.* You meet with a business that wants you to draft a private letter ruling request before it creates a tax-free loan repayment program for its employees.

Chapter 3, *Gifts and Bequests: What's Tax Got to Do with It?* You are asked to create a term sheet for a family business that is being restructured to start passing the business on to the next generation.

Chapter 4, *Benefits: Tax Is Not on the Fringe.* A client is being audited, and you must draft a protest letter to get an appeal.

Chapter 5, *Deductions: Deducing When It's Deductible.* You are asked to draft sections of a Tax Court petition to challenge the IRS's results of an audit by comparing your client's facts to case law.

Chapter 6, *Depreciation: Recapturing the Love of Tax.* In preparation for a business negotiation, you must draft a bullet point memorandum explaining the consequences of sales of various machines.

Chapter 7, *Accounting: There's a Method to the Madness.* You are asked to draft a tax opinion regarding the sale of a business's subsidiary.

Chapter 8, *Gains: It's Capital to Advise You.* You must draft a letter to a client regarding the tax treatment of the sale of various properties.

Chapter 9, *Exchanges: Do You Like the Results?* You are asked to draft an email explaining the tax consequences of a proposed exchange of property your client wants to qualify as a like-kind exchange.

Chapter 10, *Divorce: Breaking up Is So Taxing*. After meeting with a client, you must revise the tax sections of a divorce agreement.

Chapter 11, *EITC: Earning Praise for Your Simplicity*. You must draft a one-page flier explaining the Earned Income Tax Credit to a group that a local nonprofit is trying to help.

Chapter 12, *Tax-Exempts: Asking Nicely Not to Pay Tax*. You are tasked with preparing a portion of an application to form a 501(c)(3).

Chapter 13, *Civil Litigation: I Won—and the Government Won*. You are advising on a negotiation before your client proceeds in civil litigation.

Client counseling, legal drafting, negotiation, and advocacy are the core skills of the legal profession. *Developing Professional Skills: Income Taxation* provides you opportunities to develop those skills.

Table of Contents

Developing Professional Skills:

INCOME TAXATION

CHAPTER ONE

Income

It's Great, Not Gross

As you eagerly pack your bag to go home from work, a partner at your firm, Russell Socio, comes in and asks if you have time to talk to a new client, Simone Prime. Simone is a friend of Russell's. You tell Russell you would be happy to stay and meet Simone.

A middle-aged woman in tidy clothes walks into your office and takes a seat. The woman seems agitated and does not want to look you in the eye. You begin the conversation:

You: Hello, Ms. Prime. It's nice to meet you. Have you known Russell for long?

Simone: Please call me Simone. Russell and I went to high school together, but then our paths diverged.

You: What do you do now, Simone?

Simone: I operate a restaurant, Le Canard Jaune.

You: I know that restaurant. It has amazing food and the best service.

Simone: Thank you. John Cuisinier is the chef and, as you know, he's absolutely amazing. And I could never replace my wait staff.

Simone has run the restaurant for five years. She has ten employees who work in the kitchen and thirty employees who work in the front of the house. They are a very close group of people, and Simone considers it her job to take care of her employees.

You want to know more about the restaurant, and whether this representation will necessitate a visit and, perhaps, dinner. You wait to ask that question until you can ascertain whether the representation of Simone would present a conflict with your representation of existing clients. You ask Simone about other parties involved with her restaurant, including suppliers, vendors, or other people she owes money. Simone provides you a list and your assistant performs a preliminary conflict check against existing clients and matters. This preliminary check indicates that you may represent Simone, although you need to discuss the terms of the engagement letter with Simone. For now, you feel comfortable proceeding with the discussion and finding out more about her problem.

Simone explains that she is worried because she has been paying several of her employees under the table. She tells you that these employees prefer this type of arrangement. They receive their payments in cash immediately rather than having to wait for pay periods. She has quite a bit of turnover for the lowest paid jobs, and she thinks of them like Uber drivers. You recognize that she's arguing they are independent contractors.

As you scribble down notes, you ask Simone whether this arrangement applies to all employees or only a subset. You are not surprised to hear that it is only to a small group. The chef gets paid an annual salary that is competitive for the market plus she started letting him stay in an apartment over the restaurant since his recent divorce. He has not been in a good emotional place and has not wanted to find a new place to live.

For the front room staff, Simone tells you that she pays them an amount of cash that does not sound like a lot of money to you. When you ask her, she tells you that she also gives them food from the kitchen for themselves and their families.

As Simone is speaking, your assistant comes in and reminds you of a dinner meeting you have. You apologize to Simone and explain that you need to attend a previously scheduled meeting. You suggest that Simone schedule another meeting for the end of the week, at which point you hope to have a formal conflict clearance and engagement letter for Simone to sign. She asks if you will be able to give her some guidance on how to proceed with her employees. You respond that you will do your best.

Before you leave for your meeting, you pull up the language of section 119 that you are pretty sure will be relevant:

Section 119. Meals or lodging furnished for the convenience of the employer.

(a) Meals and lodging furnished to employee, his spouse, and his dependents, pursuant to employment. There shall be excluded from gross income of an employee the value of any meals or lodging furnished to him, his spouse, or any of his dependents by or on behalf of his employer for the convenience of the employer, but only if—

(1) in the case of meals, the meals are furnished on the business premises of the employer, or

(2) in the case of lodging, the employee is required to accept such lodging on the business premises of his employer as a condition of his employment. . . .

(b) Special rules. . . .

(4) Meals furnished to employees on business premises where meals of most employees are otherwise excludable. All meals furnished on the business premises of an employer to such employer's employees shall be treated as furnished for the convenience of the employer if, without regard to this paragraph, more than half of the employees to whom such meals are furnished on such premises are furnished such meals for the convenience of the employer.

Writing Assignment:

Your next day is light, so you begin preparing for the meeting with Simone. You realize that you have several significant issues to discuss with her. You take a deep breath and begin methodically preparing a talking point outline so that you don't miss anything, can think through what to do next, and will be able to discuss the matter with Russell.

Client Counseling Outline:

Attorney Name:
Client:
Date:

Who is involved in the new matter?

What **facts** do you know now that are relevant to the matter?

As described by the client?

As perceived by you?

What do you see are the **legal issues or problems** in the matter?

What are your **next steps** to address the potential problems?

What questions should you ask your client?

What legal research should you do?

Points to Consider:

1. Does it matter that you are representing Simone at little to no cost?
2. Can you limit your representation to the tax issues or will you become her general counselor?
3. Can you discuss all of these issues in the next meeting? How should you prioritize your time?

Optional Research:

What does the IRS tell the public are the common law rules for determining who is an employee and who is an independent contractor?

CHAPTER TWO

Loans

Forgiveness Is Tax-Free

While busily finishing up a client counseling outline, another partner in your firm, Maggie Rhodes, walks into your office and hands you a file. The file contains some handwritten notes. Rhodes explains that the HunterAcademic company recently hired the firm to work through its plan to set up a loan repayment program for their employees whereby HunterAcademic will pay off employees' student loans.

HunterAcademic is not sure of what, if anything, it needs to do before starting to pay off the loans. Rhodes tells you that she wants to get a private letter ruling (PLR) for HunterAcademic to ensure that the payment plan does not generate income for its employees because, as you are aware, the default is that loan forgiveness generates gross income.

You have heard of HunterAcademic. It is in the business of providing financial literacy education to underserved communities. Its employees are well-educated in business but choose a significantly lower-paying job in order to give back to society.

Rhodes is optimistic that you will be able to secure the PLR which will guarantee the tax result, both for HunterAcademic and its employees. Without a PLR, the repayment could later be found to be taxable compensation to the employees, and Rhodes does not think that HunterAcademic should assume this risk because of the negative publicity that would result if it did.

You respect HunterAcademic's work, and you ask Rhodes how you can help. She explains that she needs you to: (1) draft a letter to the IRS requesting a PLR after confirming exactly what information will be needed in the letter, and (2) compile a list of information that you will need in order to make the request. You think of your class discussion of *Old Colony Trust v. Commissioner*, 279 U.S. 719 (1929), and section 108. You know that this will require some real effort on your part.

You review the file and note the following information in Rhodes's handwriting regarding HunterAcademic's plan:

- HunterAcademic is a 501(c)(3) serving state ____
- It provides a wide range of services, including providing financial literacy education at tax-exempt schools and community centers, serving as an information source on financial literacy and financial education, providing training and workforce development, and advocating for greater training in this area
- To increase its ability to provide this education, HunterAcademic wants to ease its employees' educational debt burdens so that more people with training in financial literacy will choose to work in underserved communities
- HunterAcademic takes a broad definition of educational loans as from both government and private sources for undergraduate and graduate studies
- Workers will sign a contract to work three years in return for loan forgiveness of up to $30,000 per year; HunterAcademic prepays educational loans and workers have their new loans forgiven as they work off their debt
- If a worker does not complete the contract, they owe HunterAcademic for its loans at a penalty rate and interest instead of owing on the discharged student loans

Before you can draft a letter to the IRS, you find a form in the file. You know that you have to fill in the following details.

__________, ____

Internal Revenue Service
Associate Chief Counsel Income Tax and Accounting

Attn: Box 14095
Benjamin Franklin Station
Washington, DC 20044

Dear Sir or Madame,

The taxpayer, HunterAcademic, requests a ruling on whether. . . .

A. Statement of facts.

   1. Taxpayer information.

   2. Description of taxpayers, business operations.

   3. Facts relating to transaction.

B. Ruling requested.

C. Statement of law.

D. Analysis.

E. Conclusion.

Writing Assignment:

Before you can begin to draft the letter, you must find from the client the information that the letter requires. List the questions you will ask the client in the order that you think they should be asked. You must submit the list in writing for Rhodes's review, so the list must be clear. It may help you decide the types of facts you need if you think about what the government is likely to be worried about with this program.

QUESTIONS FOR HunterAcademic TO CLARIFY THE FACTS:

1.

2.

3.

4.

Points to Consider:

1. Should you discuss the operational workings of the loan repayment program or limit yourself to legal concerns?
2. What downsides are there of filing for a PLR?
3. Does Rhodes or the client decide to file for a PLR?

Optional Research:

The IRS updates a Revenue Procedure each year with detailed instructions for the public on how to file a request for a PLR. Locate this year's Revenue Procedure and the section of that Procedure that gives general instructions for the request.

CHAPTER THREE

Gifts and Bequests

What's Tax Got to Do with It?

Your firm has represented Knut Boats for a long time. Knut Boats is a business that makes small leisure crafts. Because the business is family-owned and operated by a married couple, the firm also represents the couple personally. You are in your estate planning rotation and have been asked to join in helping the owners begin to transition the business to the next generation.

The business was started and run by Alice and David Merriweather. The business operates as an LLC taxable as a partnership; therefore, the owners report on their personal tax returns the income, gain, deductions, and loss generated by the business. The business was worth approximately $240 million on January 1, of this year, and there should be no significant changes to the valuation this year. Looking at the files, you see that the business has complied with all applicable business law-related rules and currently has only one class of ownership interests.

As of January 1, Knut Boats is owned 50% by Alice and 50% by David. Alice and David tell you in your initial meeting that they want to share ownership and responsibility with their children and grandchildren as Alice wants to reduce her role in the business. Alice gives you a sketch of the family tree.

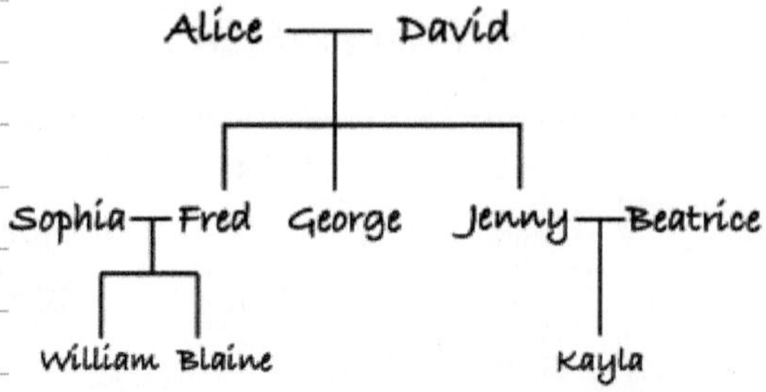

You see that she and David have three children: Fred, George, and Jenny. Fred is married to Sophia, and they have two children, William and Blaine. Jenny is married to Beatrice, and they have one child, Kayla. George has remained single.

Alice and David agree that David will retain 30% and Alice 25% after the restructuring. They want each of their children, Fred, George, and Jenny, to get 15%.

After your initial meeting but before completing the initial transfer, David died leaving his shares to Alice. Alice now wants to complete that plan and then for each of her children's families to get one-quarter of her remaining interests and for her to retain one-quarter, which she plans to leave to a charitable foundation when she dies. She would like your assistance in this transition. To keep straight what percentage each person will have, you think of the initial planned transfer as Step 1 and the transfer planned after David's death as Step 2.

For Step 2, Alice wants to create different classes of interests with Class A interests having voting rights and Class B without voting rights. Although she wants to keep values transferred in Step 2 equal as among her children, she wants these shares to be owned by her grandchildren but she does not want them to have a vote. She is thinking of splitting Fred's share one-half to each of his children. She will give Jenny's share to her one child. George will get his quarter in a trust for any future children.

She is thinking about putting limitations on the interests, such as restricting their transferability or ability to be used as collateral, to reduce the value of the interests because she's heard that might reduce her gift taxes. Alice also wants George and Jenny to contribute some amount financially to the business. Finally, Alice wants to limit operating distributions but wants to ensure that George, Jenny, and Blaine get a paid if they do work for the business.

Alice tells you that Fred is an artist who did not complete college; George is a lawyer and represents himself with respect to all of his personal matters; and Jenny is an investment banker and eager to apply her skills to the family business. Of the next generation, William wants to become a professional surfer but has yet to win anything; Blaine looks up to his aunt and is becoming a banker; and Layla is in her eighth year of undergraduate study in eighteenth century French literature.

You have looked into the taxation of gifts before, so you are familiar with the basic rules of section 102. You need to think about the impact of the transfer taxes as a general matter, although if the plan develops, you will want to speak with a partner who deals with those taxes in particular.

Writing Assignment:

The partner you are working with asks that you create a term sheet to make the information as clear as possible to the family members. You put in the term(s) column the issues that the parties should address (such as the number of interests, voting powers, management, transferability of interests), and put in the comment column the client's proposal in clear, and yet brief, language. For terms you do not yet have comments, put "[to be determined]." It is a skill to determine the number and types of issues that should be identified; four is not a magic number for this fact pattern.

TERM SHEET	
Term(s)	**Comment(s)**
1.	
2.	
3.	
4.	

Points to Consider:

1. Does anyone owe tax as a result of this transfer of interests?
2. Are there concerns outside of your expertise as a lawyer that you should raise with your client?
3. Can you represent Alice, Knut Boats, and the recipients of interests in Step 1 and Step 2?

Optional Research:

What does the IRS say regarding the valuation of closely-held corporations? It has issued a Revenue Ruling on point.

CHAPTER FOUR

Benefits

Tax Is Not on the Fringe

One of your favorite clients is a business that makes dog treats. Dr. Bertie Lee is a scientist by training, and she left a huge company making a wide range of personal health/personal care items to open a small company, Bertie's Best: Dogs' Goods For Good Dogs. Bertie's Best makes environmentally-friendly dog food, treats, and toys. Her ability to please canine friends has helped her develop a vibrant business.

Dr. Lee began the business in her kitchen and garage, but it has since grown to be a leader of all things dog-related in the U.S. She manufactures all her inventory in the U.S. and has all her employees here because she has found this is her biggest market.

Dr. Lee treats her employees well because she thinks doing so encourages them to devote significant personal effort to the business. She allows management to use the corporate jet, both to travel for business meetings as well as for personal travel. She gives all employees a 50% discount on everything the business produces. She offers free doggy daycare while employees are working. She offers doggy medical insurance to help ensure the long-term health of her employees' pets.

Dr. Lee recently received a preliminary notice of deficiency (a 30-day letter), and the IRS included a copy of the revenue agency's report that explained in detail its challenges. The issue for Bertie's Best is the employee tax it owes on the listed items. The IRS based its estimates on comparable services when appropriate:

- the use of the corporate jet for personal travel is not an excludable fringe benefit because use of the jet was not sold to customers and this discriminated in favor of highly compensated employees (§ 132(a), (h)); therefore, the $60,000 value of the flights was taxable to employees;
- the 50% discount was 10% greater than the business's 40% gross profit percentage per § 132(c); therefore, since the total value of the discount was $42,000 this year, $4,200 should have been included in employees' income;
- the dog-related benefits are not an excludible fringe benefit so that the fair market value of these goods was taxable to employees, including the doggy daycare used by 28 employees at a cost of $20 per day, five days per week, for 48 weeks per year, which is $134,400, and the doggy medical insurance valued at $2000 times 25 employees, which is $50,000; and
- there are income tax and employment tax consequences to the employees as well; the IRS will be following up with Bertie's Best's employees.

Dr. Lee surprises you with her level of frustration with the IRS. First, she argues:

- the $60,000 of flights included both personal and work-related travel as at least half of the flights were for people who worked on the flight or met with stores at the destination;
- the IRS miscalculated the business's gross profit percentage as last year the aggregate sales price was $900,000 and the aggregate cost was $441,000; and
- the doggy daycare and doggy medical insurance clearly improved her employees' productivity.

Then Dr. Lee asks you to work it out so that all of her employees' wages are converted to fringe benefits. She is happy to provide them housing, food, clothing, anything they might choose because she believes doing so would reduce everyone's tax bills. You tell her that you need to think about the scope of this conversion.

You have been asked to prepare a protest letter, which is a prerequisite for the taxpayer to seek an agency appeal. You double-check that the audit has proceeded within the time limit, so that statute of limitations is not going to be a winning argument. You also recognize that the manner in which the protest letter is submitted primarily depends upon the amount of the tax liability in controversy. As the challenged amount for Bertie's Best exceeds $25,000 for the taxable year, the taxpayer must file a formal written protest within 30 days from the date appearing on the 30-day letter.

Writing Assignment:

After saying goodbye to Dr. Lee, you have two tasks. First, you need to respond to the 30-day letter. There is no official form for a written protest. You decide to use your firm's form included below but, for today, draft the sections regarding the statement of facts and the statement of law. Second, you must think about your response to Dr. Lee's desire to convert wages into fringe benefits, but you realize this should be a conversation in person and not in writing.

Protest Letter

Internal Revenue Service
[Address]

[Date]

Re: Taxpayer's Name
Address
T.I.N.

Dear Sir or Madam:

In response to your correspondence dated ________, asserting an income tax deficiency for the taxable year ______, this letter protests certain findings in your letter and its attached examination report (copies of which are attached).

The following information is submitted in support of this protest:

1. Appeals conference request.
The taxpayer requests an appeals conference with an officer of the IRS Appeals Division for a time convenient to both parties.

2. Taxpayer's Name, Address and Telephone Number [to come]

3. Date and Symbols of the transmittal letter [to come]

4. Taxable Years Involved
Calendar (or Fiscal) Year(s) ___________________________

5. Schedule of Contested Adjustments
[Set forth in separately itemized paragraphs the adjustments included by the examining agent in the 30-day letter (including penalty assertions) with which the taxpayer disagrees.]

6. Statement of Facts
[Set forth an organized description of the relevant facts surrounding each of the protested adjustments. Where appropriate, reference and attach affidavits and other supporting documents.]

7. Statement of Law
[Set forth the law applicable to each of the protested adjustments and apply the law to the facts of the case.]

The undersigned prepared this protest on behalf of the taxpayer but does not know personally whether the statement of facts contained in this protest is true and correct.

A Form 2848, Power of Attorney, authorizing the undersigned to represent the taxpayer in this matter, is also enclosed.

Respectfully yours,
[Representative]

Enclosures

Points to Consider:

1. What information do you need to gather from Bertie's Best before being able to finalize the protest letter?
2. What are the business issues related to providing Bertie's Best's existing forms of fringe benefits and how are they reconciled with the IRS's position on their taxation?
3. How do you proceed if your client is frustrated about receipt of a 30-day letter?

Optional Research:

What does the IRS tell its employees are the rules for when someone wants to dispute a 30-day letter by appealing to the Appeals Office? You can find this information in the Internal Revenue Manual.

CHAPTER FIVE

Deductions

Deducing When It's Deductible

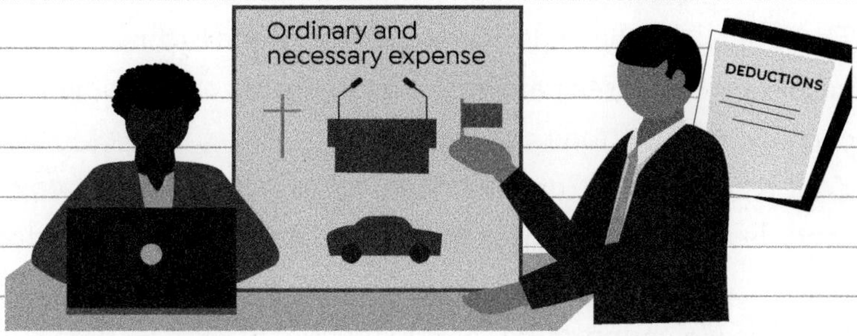

One of your clients, Samuel Costabile, came to see you after having opened a car dealership. Costabile is a minister at a local church with a significant congregation and is also the mayor of the town. He had been a salesperson at the local car dealership which recently went out of business because of bankruptcy. Costabile worried that the community was losing a big employer that had also brought in customers from surrounding communities. He wanted to open a new car dealership as a tool to bolster his town.

The main problem that Costabile initially faced was reestablishing a relationship with the car manufacturer that had been sold through the previous dealership. That particular manufacture was very popular in the community, and Costabile had been concerned that changing manufacturers would reduce his business. However, the manufacturer had been worried that the town was a bad market and the new business would not be sustainable. Therefore, the manufacturer had little interest in continuing the relationship.

Costabile paid off $37 million of the $65 million debt between the old dealership and the manufacturer to rebuild the relationship. Costabile claimed a deduction for the payment on the grounds that it was a legitimate business expense.

Costabile came to see you because he had received a 30-day letter from the IRS. Costabile isn't sure what to do and reached out to you for assistance. The letter and audit report challenges the validity of the deduction under section 162. It determines Costabile's tax deficiency is $13.23 million.

Section 162(a) provides:

There shall be allowed as a deduction all the ordinary and necessary expenses paid or incurred during the taxable year in carrying on any trade or business . . .

Your research into "ordinary and necessary expenses" compares *Welch* and *Jenkins* for purposes of the deduction available under section 162.

Welch v. Helvering, 290 U.S. 111 (1933):

- The taxpayer was secretary of the E. L. Welch Company, which had been in the grain business until it was adjudged bankrupt and had its debts discharged.
- The taxpayer began purchasing grain on a commission and, to re-establish relations with Welch Co. customers, he paid off some Welch Co. debts.
- The Court assumed the payments were necessary for the development of the petitioner's business because "we should be slow to override his judgment."
- However, the Court denied the deduction because it was not "ordinary," which the Court defined as "a variable affected by time and place and circumstance," so that ordinary can be a once in a lifetime lawsuit because lawsuits are common. Nevertheless, people do not ordinarily pay the debts of others "even though the result might be to heighten their reputation for generosity and opulence."
- The Court gave and dismissed examples of paying off thefts by a family ancestor or of getting an education to be cultured: "Reputation and learning are akin to capital assets, like the goodwill of an old partnership. For many, they are the only tools with which to hew a pathway to success. The money spent in acquiring them is well and wisely spent. It is not an ordinary expense of the operation of a business."

Jenkins v. Commissioner, T.C. Memo. 1983-667:

- Harold Jenkins, popularly known as country musician Conway Twitty, deducted under section 162 amounts he repaid to investors in his defunct fast food venture, Twitty Burger, Inc.
- The court accepted that these payments were not to protect Jenkins's investment in Twitty Burger or to revitalize the corporation.
- The court also accepted that most of Conway Twitty's motivation was based on the perceived expectations of country music fans and to protect his personal reputation and was not merely a sense of moral obligation (the latter which would not be deductible). "Country entertainers go to great lengths to protect their images, for they correctly realize that both business associates and fans judge their artistic efforts in the light of perceptions of the artist's personality, professional conduct, and moral character."
- "We conclude that there was a proximate relationship between the payments made . . . and petitioner's trade or business as a country music entertainer so as to render those payments an ordinary and necessary expense of that business."

Writing Assignment:

The partner you work for has asked you to draft sections for a Tax Court petition using the form below (included to permit you to see what you will ultimately be writing for the partner). For today, as your first step, the partner tells you to write (1) one paragraph containing the argument why the IRS erred, (2) one paragraph containing the facts upon which you base this argument, and (3) a list of no more than three questions you would like to ask the client.

Tax Court Petition

Samuel Costabile,
Petitioner

V.

Commissioner of Internal Revenue,
Respondent.

Petition

The Petitioner hereby petitions for a redetermination of the deficiency set forth by the Commissioner of Internal Revenue in his Notice of Deficiency (bearing symbols "__:__ __:__") dated _________, 20__, and as a basis, for the petitioner's case alleges as follows:

1. The Petitioner has a legal residence at __________. Petitioner's taxpayer identification number is ___________. The return for the tax year ending December 31, 20__ was filed with the office of Internal Revenue Service at _________, ___.

2. The Notice of Deficiency for the tax year ending December 31, 20__ (a copy of which is attached hereto and marked as exhibit "A") was mailed to the Petitioner on or after ______, 20__, and was issued by the office of the Internal Revenue Service at _________, ___.

3. The deficiency as determined by the Commissioner is an income tax and additions to tax pursuant to the Internal Revenue Code section 6662 as:

Tax Year Ended	Deficiency	Additions to tax IRC Section 6662(a)
________	________	________

[all of which] is in dispute.

4. The determination of addition to tax set forth in the Notice of Deficiency is based upon the following errors:

A. The Commissioner erred in determining that petitioner received. . . .

B. [And more as needed.]

5. The facts upon which the petitioner relies as the basis for his case:

A. The Petitioner. . . .

B. [And more as needed.]

WHEREFORE, it is prayed that the Court hear this case and determine that there is no deficiency and no addition to tax due from Petitioner for the taxable year of 20__.

Dated: ___________, 20__

By:
Attorney for petitioner
Address
Telephone
Attorney number

[Attachments omitted.]

Points to Consider:

1. Why do you need to gather additional information from Costabile?
2. What additional legal research would you want to perform?
3. Do you have to disclose uncomfortable facts in your petition?

Optional Research:

What does the Tax Court say is the required form of taxpayer filings? (The Tax Court issues its own rules for appearing before the court.)

CHAPTER SIX

Depreciation

Recapturing the Love of Tax

Gregor Malkovich is the chief executive officer of Super Widgets of America Corp. (SWAC). SWAC is a business that produces widgets. Malkovich believes that the company has acquired too many widget presses and is considering selling some of those machines.

You have known Malkovich for many years, and you recognize that he is concerned SWAC is losing money and market share. He is facing stiff competition from volume discount retailers and online distributors of widgets.

Malkovich believes he can sell some of the widget presses to Nick Dylan at Seminal Emergence Corp. (SEC), which is just starting a division making widgets. The following email is the latest correspondence on this potential sale:

Purchase of widget presses

Gregor:

As discussed, SEC is willing to purchase two widget presses at $1 million per machine. However, we need to know these are still in good working condition. The transaction will be subject to all the customary representations, warrantees, covenants, and conditions. We anticipate sending you a term sheet by the end of the week.

Sincerely, Nick

You know that SWAC's many presses are different, so you ask how Malkovich is going to decide which ones to sell. He wants to tell SEC that the older machines are better because recent regulatory changes for producers of the newer machines made the machines less efficient. You are not certain when the regulatory changes came out; you thought that they were still pending.

Malkovich gives you the following chart of his machines:

Machine ID	Acquired	Cost	Today's basis	Fair market value
68234015	9/1/12	$750,300	$0	$823,634
72119852	2/3/15	$890,500	$0	$998,323
82339442	11/9/19	$1,640,222	$0	$931,135
95924311	8/16/21	$2,021,000	$0	$976,234
96034521	1/23/23	$1,750,100	$299,985	$1,231,000

You do some research and feel comfortable that you understand the rules of expensing and bonus and accelerated depreciation. You also review your notes on the rules on depreciation recapture:

> Depreciable property's basis is reduced (eventually to $0) as a result of depreciation, but that depreciation may not reflect a reduction in its fair market value. As a result, a depreciated property's basis may be less than its fair market value. If this occurs, there may be gain on a sale that exists only because previous depreciation deductions reduced the taxpayer's basis in the asset.
>
> Because depreciation deductions offset ordinary income, Congress enacted section 1245 and 1250. These sections call the gain associated with basis lowered by depreciation below original basis "recapture," and that gain is taxed at ordinary rates. Example: you buy an asset for $10M cost basis; reduce its basis to $1M because of depreciation deductions; sell the asset for $7M; you have $6M of recapture taxed at ordinary income rates. This matters from a tax perspective because the normal character of gain on such a sale is at lower capital gain rates.
>
> A sale of a depreciated asset may produce two types of gain: recapture gain taxed as ordinary income and gain in excess of original cost basis taxed at lower capital gain rates. Example: you buy an asset for $10M cost basis; reduce its basis to $1M because of depreciation deductions; sell the asset for $12M (caused by a shortage of assets); you have $9M of recapture taxed at ordinary income rates and $2M taxed at capital gain rates.

Writing Assignment:

Malkovich wants you to write him a short bullet point memorandum explaining the tax consequences of selling each of the five machines. You use Malkovich's billing partner's preferred form given below, which focuses on being concise as to your conclusions. You also need to plan for how you will present this information to opposing counsel. At this point that planning does not have to be in writing, but you should be prepared to discuss your ideas with Malkovich.

Memorandum

To:
From:
Re:
Date:

With respect to the sale of two widget presses for $1 million each to SEC, below are my findings regarding each of the five machines you have considered:

- ID 68234015:
- ID 72119852:
- ID 82339442:
- ID 95924311:
- ID 96034521:

Additional points that we should discuss:

-

Finally, I would like to discuss recommendations at your convenience.

Points to Consider:

1. What can Malkovich and/or you say about the quality of the machines and the regulations on their producers?
2. How would you balance the tax and business consequences of selling a particular machine?
3. What other factors with respect to the machines do you want to investigate before negotiations with SEC?

Optional Research:

What form is used to report depreciation recapture to the IRS?

CHAPTER SEVEN

Accounting

There's a Method to the Madness

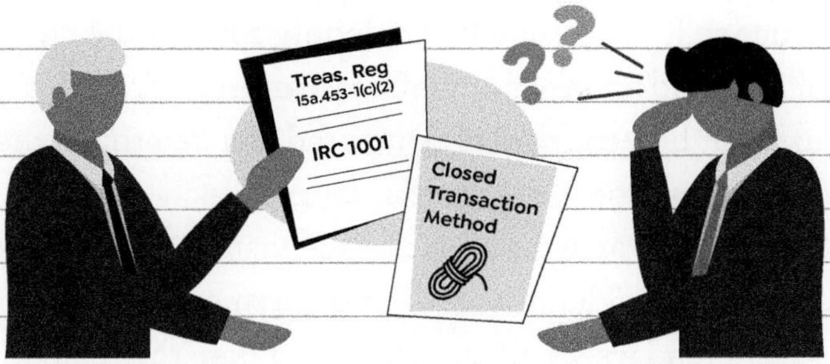

Climber LLC is a large producer of climbing equipment. Climber LLC's managing member is Bob Harness, and he owns 60% of the LLC's interests. You've known Harness for many years.

Harness tells you the bad news that Climber LLC needs to sell one of its subsidiaries, Rocky Mountain Vacations, LLC ("Rocky Mountain"). It is not that Climber LLC wants to downsize but, with recent market changes, it needs to sell its interest in Rocky Mountain for increased liquidity.

A recent press release tells at least part of the story:

> **Don't expect to climb Montana** with Climber LLC. Earthbound Trips Inc. has offered to buy Climber LLC's vacation package business for $50 million.

Most of Climber LLC's owners are excited about the transaction, but Harness recognizes that Earthbound is going to impose its own limits on the deal. Harness hands you an early version of the term sheet that Earthbound has proposed. You see that the key is how much and when Climber LLC will be paid:

> Buyer will transfer to Seller some amount in cash ("Consideration"). The Consideration will be paid in three tranches:
>
> - $25 million is to be paid on the Closing Date;
> - $15 million is to be paid one year after the Closing Date to the extent that Target meets the Earning Threshold; and

- 10% of net profits received in the third, fourth, and fifth years after the Closing Date to the extent that Target meets the Earning Threshold.

You notice that the payments are highly conditional on the ongoing business and an as-yet-undefined Earning Threshold. You also recognize that how the deal is structured will determine the tax treatment of this contingent obligation.

You do some research and see that the installment method most often applies when consideration is a set of payments over a period of years. You first read a secondary source and then the regulations accompanying section 453 on the installment method. Because the maximum selling price is unknown but there is a set date by which all payments will be made, Treasury Regulation 15a.453-1(c)(2) applies. The principle that drives the rule is that the taxpayer should only be required to account for cash proceeds in the year they are realized with basis recovery spread out over time for potential additional consideration.

You discuss this over the phone with Harness, and he is not happy. Climber LLC has a $42 million basis in its interests in Rocky Mountain that would not be recovered in the year of the initial sale, and it will take five years to recover all of the basis. Additionally, you have to explain to him a deferred interest payment in section 453A that Climber LLC will have to pay on the deferred tax liability.

An alternative method of accounting you could use is the closed transaction method of section 1001. Harness likes it much better. If the taxpayer elects this method, the taxpayer pays tax on the cash received in the year of the transaction plus the fair market value of contingent obligations. Fair market value is not defined in the statute but is widely accepted as the price at which a buyer would be willing to purchase the contingent obligation in an arm's length transaction. Harness tells you that an appraiser would say the fair market value of the contingent obligation at the closing date is $25 million. Under this method, the taxpayer can fully recover basis in the year of the transaction, and there is no interest payable for deferred payments. The downside includes the requirement that the taxpayer pay tax on the fair market value of the contingent obligation even though such payments may never materialize and without the possibility of a later deduction if there is no payment.

Harness needs a tax opinion to give to the other voting members of Climbers LLC to persuade them that his plan under section 1001 will work. Therefore, your firm needs to give him an opinion with an appropriate level of comfort to assure him and the other members of the likelihood that his preferred tax treatment will be respected by the IRS. This level of comfort tells him whether it will be/should be/more likely than not will be treated a certain way by the IRS. An opinion letter has the backing of your law firm; and, therefore, you risk malpractice if what you say does not prove to be accurate.

Writing Assignment:

To start the draft opinion, you need to draft language for the facts section giving the facts that you think are necessary for your opinion, your level of comfort in the opinion section, and a description of the law on which you rely for the law and analysis sections. You have the firm's form for opinions below. You recognize this is a big opportunity to establish yourself within the law firm.

Draft Tax Opinion

[Client]

__________, __

Ladies and Gentlemen:

You have requested the opinion (the "Opinion") of ____________ (the "Firm") as to whether the sale of 100% of the interests of Rocky Mountain Vacations, LLC ("Target") to Earthbound Trips Inc. ("Buyer") by Climber LLC ("Seller") in return for contingent consideration pursuant to the Agreement dated _______, ____ (the "Agreement") can elect to be taxable as a closed transaction pursuant to section 1001 of the Internal Revenue Code of 1986, as amended (the "Code"). For purposes of the Opinion set forth below, we have read and relied upon the copies or originals, certified or otherwise identified, including all schedules and exhibits attached thereto of the Agreement.

I. Facts

This Opinion is based on the following facts disclosed by Seller to the Firm and, to the extent they were materially inaccurate, the conclusions reached in this Opinion might be adversely affected.

1. ____________________
2. ____________________

II. Opinion

Based on our review and subject to the facts as set forth in paragraph I above and the qualifications to, and limitations on, the validity and effectiveness of the Opinion expressed in paragraph IV below, the Firm opines that the sale contemplated by the Agreement following a proper election [<u>level of comfort</u>] constitute a sale within the provisions of Section 1001.

III. Law and Analysis

____

IV. Caveats and Limitations

The Opinion of the Firm expressed in paragraph II above is subject to the following qualifications to, and limitations on, its validity and effectiveness:

1. The Opinion is limited to the tax issues specifically addressed in the Opinion.
2. The Opinion set forth in paragraph II above is based upon the Internal Revenue Code and its legislative history, Treasury Regulations, judicial decisions, and current administrative rulings and practices of the IRS, all as in effect on the date of this Opinion. These authorities may be amended or revoked at any time. Any changes may or may not be retroactive.
3. This Opinion does not address any state, local, foreign, or other tax consequences that may result from any of the transactions. This Opinion is addressed solely to Seller and may not be relied upon by any other party to this transaction or in any other transaction without our prior written consent.
4. This Opinion is based upon the representations, documents, facts, and assumptions that have been included or referenced herein and the assumptions that such information is accurate, true, and authentic. In the event any one of the facts or assumptions is incorrect, in whole or in part, the conclusions reached in this Opinion might be adversely affected.

Points to Consider:

1. What should you do if you disagree with Harness as to the better tax classification of the transaction?
2. What should your client understand with respect to the cost of his chosen transaction?
3. How can this opinion help prevent future conflicts?

Optional Research:

What is the Treasury Regulation's difference between "substantial authority" and "more likely than not" levels of comfort to avoid tax penalties?

CHAPTER EIGHT

Gains

It's Capital to Advise You

You came back from a late lunch feeling very happy with life. Waiting at your office is a partner, Peter McCartney, and two people, one of whom looks like an important client and the other is almost certainly her daughter. Peter introduces you to Maria Rolliando and her daughter, Diana. Maria has used the firm for many years. Peter thinks you are ready to handle this matter—which you understand is a big honor but also a lot of pressure.

You thank Peter and ask Maria and Diana to join you in your office. You wish Peter were joining you, but he has another meeting to attend.

You ask Maria and Diana how you can help. Maria tells you that it is really Diana who has the question, but that Maria will be paying the legal bills. As Maria uses the firm for many things, she wants your bill added to her tab. You tell her that you'll have to check with Peter about the logistics but that you can gather more information now.

Diana: I am in negotiations to sell 1,350 shares this year for $560 per share.

You: That sounds good. What is the stock and when did you acquire it?

Diana: I received the stock from my boss, Brett Locatiger, late last year.

You (you recognize this business is Locatiger, the newest online delivery platform): Was the stock compensation?

Diana: Yes, it had been a really tough year, but we've made major improvements with our algorithm for deliveries that has really helped Locatiger stock.

You: What was it worth when you received the stock?

Diana: Only $23.50 per share.

You: That is amazing upside! When you received the stock, were you able to trade it immediately or were there any restrictions?

Diana: I wasn't able to trade it for six months. My accountant had me make a section 83(b) election. Now I'm ready to sell the stock because I'm worried about Brett.

You focus on the tax consequences, although you are curious about Brett and want to touch base with a securities lawyer about insider trading. Diana tells you that she thinks the tax bill on the sale is going to be big and that she doesn't want to have to pay any more tax on the stock. She says she's already paid tax. You realize that she does not recognize that she only paid tax on the stock's value when she received it and has never paid tax on its appreciation.

You take a deep breath and ask Diana if there is anything else, as your mind races over how to break the news about the taxable gain. Diana then tells you that she is going to sell either some land she's been holding or an apartment building, neither of which were as good of an investment as the stock. You ask for some details about the land and the apartment.

Diana had purchased beachfront property as an investment for $1,960,000 several years ago. The land has suffered from climate change (it's now flooded), and she thinks she can get $725,000 for it. She purchased the apartment building in February of this year as an investment for $14.3 million, but it turns out to have structural damage and needs a sizable investment that Diana does not want to make. Without the investment, she thinks she can only get $10.95 million for the building.

You thank Diana for all of the information as you furiously scribble down notes. You tell her that you'll follow up with Peter about billing and get back to her and Maria. You know you need to think over what she has told you.

As they stand up to leave, you ask one more time if there is anything else you should know about Diana's recent investments. She tells you as an offhand remark that she received $24,350 in dividends this year and got $6.75 million on the sale of a painting her grandmother had painted and given her in 2020. Diana was thrilled to make the profit, knowing it would have made her grandmother proud, but sadly her grandmother died in 2024.

Writing Assignment:

You see Peter in the elevator and want to run through the facts but there is not enough time. He asks you to prepare a draft letter to send to the client. You use the firm's form letter below.

Advisory Letter

Tax Law Firm, LLP
2925 Law Firm Rd.
City, State 00000

[____________________, 20__]

Confidential Attorney-Client Communications

Via Electronic Mail
Diana Rolliando
1500 Ivy Street
City, State 00000

Re: Selling Properties in [20__]

Dear Ms. Rolliando,

You have asked our firm to evaluate your options for selling property this year. You have provided us with the basic information regarding your situation and your objectives for disposing of several pieces of property discussed individually below. Accordingly, this letter summarizes: (1) the consequences of selling the stock, land, an apartment building, and a painting; and (2) our preliminary recommendation based on the facts you have provided to date.

1. Sale of the stock:

2. Sale of the land:

3. Sale of the apartment building:

4. Sale of the painting:

Preliminary recommendation:

I look forward to discussing these alternatives with you. Please do not hesitate to call me with any questions or comments.

Sincerely,

Points to Consider:

1. How much detail regarding capital gains policy and law do you need to discuss with Diana?
2. Can you discuss all of these issues with Diana while Maria is in the room? Does it matter that Maria is paying for your legal fees and expenses?
3. How comfortable do you need to be at math to give tax advice?

Optional Research:

If the painting was not given directly to Diana but held in an irrevocable grantor trust not included in the deceased grantor's gross estate for federal estate tax purposes, would the painting receive the step-up in basis pursuant to section 1014? The IRS has issued a Revenue Ruling on point.

CHAPTER NINE

Exchanges

Do You Like the Results?

You have a new client, Liz Darcy, that you met through a friend. Darcy told you in your first meeting that she bought a shopping mall in March 2024 for $4.25 million. The building now has a $3.38 million basis and the land a $614,000 basis. She just received a $6.2 million appraisal for the mall; however, Darcy thinks that the market is going to suffer in the near term. Although she tells you she wants out of the investment, she does not want to be saddled with a large tax bill, and she wants her investment closer to her home in Bloomington, ___.

You discussed with Darcy a like-kind exchange in which Darcy could exchange the mall for another piece of investment property. One of the partners you work with, Chuck Axelrod, arranges a lot of these types of transactions. Darcy is excited about the ability to defer tax and get out of the mall.

Darcy calls you to tell you that she has the ideal property to exchange for her own. It's an apartment building in Bloomington owned by Carl Bromer. You know Bromer's lawyer, Fred MacIntyre, from law school, and you have read about how Bromer bought the apartment building earlier this year for $6.4 million, but it has been declining in value for several years because it needs some upkeep. You have also seen in the news that Bromer has had a very good year with his investments.

Darcy is planning on going out of the country next Wednesday on a month-long vacation, and she will be out of pocket until she gets back. She hopes to transfer out of the mall business before she goes, but she's worried about logistics. Bromer also travels frequently, and he is out of the country and will be gone again when Darcy returns.

You have done a little work with like-kind exchanges and remember that there is an important safe harbor in Revenue Procedure 2000-37 as modified by Revenue Procedure 2004-51. In them the IRS has agreed not to challenge "parking transactions" whereby a replacement property is transferred to a third-party facilitator before the contracts are entered into for the exchange of the taxpayer's relinquished property. You have the following notes:

Treas. Reg. § 1.1031(k)–1(a) provides a "deferred exchange" is an exchange in which the taxpayer transfers property held for productive use in a trade or business or for investment (the "relinquished property") and subsequently receives property to be held either for productive use in a trade or business or for investment (the "replacement property").

- *Must have written agreement.*
- *Replacement property must be identified before the end of the identification period ("identification period") and received before the end of the exchange period ("exchange period").*
    - *The identification period begins on the date the taxpayer transfers the relinquished property and ends at midnight on the 45th day thereafter.*
    - *The exchange period begins on the date the taxpayer transfers the relinquished property and ends at midnight on the earlier of the 180th day thereafter or the due date (including extensions) for the taxpayer's income tax return for which the transfer of the relinquished property occurs.*

Revenue Procedure 2000-37 provides a safe harbor that the IRS will not challenge a § 1031 exchange if the property is held in a "qualified exchange accommodation arrangement" (QEAA).

- *A QEAA is a third-party U.S. taxpayer that temporarily holds relinquished or replacement property to increase flexibility in the timing of sales.*
- *The QEAA must be treated as the beneficial owner of the property for all federal income tax purposes, and all parties must report the federal income tax attributes of the property on their tax returns consistent with the agreement.*
- *Modified by Rev. Proc. 2004-51: the safe harbor does not apply if the taxpayer owned replacement property within the 180-day period before initiating a QEAA (i.e., can't exchange your own replacement property for your own relinquished property, presumably to switch basis).*

Writing Assignment:

You need to draft Darcy an email explaining the tax consequences of the like-kind exchange. You need to include requests for the information that you need to gather. As you are reviewing your draft, Bromer leaves you a message because he has heard through back channels about Darcy's desire to switch properties.

Draft Email Response

To:
CC:
From:
Subject:

Liz:

Regarding the potential like-kind exchange of a mall that you bought in March 2024 for an apartment building currently owned by Carl Bromer . . . .

We should get more information before you leave, specifically. . . .

Points to Consider:

1. How do you decide how much detail to give your client on the Revenue Procedure, Regulation, and statute?
2. How do you identify any additional information that might help your client?
3. How can you respond to Bromer's call?

Optional Research:

In a reverse like-kind exchange suggested by Revenue Procedure 2000-37, does the Tax Court always impose the 45/180 day tests?

CHAPTER TEN

Divorce

Breaking up Is So Taxing

Your law firm requires you to rotate among their many different groups so that you can see a variety of clients. For the next couple months you are in family planning. Consequently, you are not surprised when Cameron Mathews was escorted into your office. You were surprised that Cameron was dabbing her eyes. Law school did not prepare you to deal with what is clearly going to be an emotional meeting. Grabbing your box of tissues, you welcome her into your office and ask her to sit.

Cameron tells you that she has been married for seven years and has two children. Marie is five and Blake is three. Her spouse, Kimberly, earns more than she does and has been managing their money. Cameron works as a nurse earning $48,000 per year and Kimberly works as an investment advisor and earned $150,000 last year. However, Kimberly's compensation changes pretty radically each year. They have been separated for over a year, but both continue to live in their historic home for financial reasons and for the sake of the children. Cameron wants a cheap divorce and full custody of the children.

Looking discomfited, Cameron then tries to slip in that she came to see you first because she knows that your specialty is taxation. She is worried about their taxes because she has never really been a part of that decision making. She just signs when and where Kimberly tells her.

You assure her that this is pretty common and ask her if there is anything in particular she is worried about. Cameron tells you that she doesn't think they filed last year but requested an extension, which she believes is coming up soon. Also, they recently received a letter from the IRS, but she hasn't read it.

Beginning to rush, Cameron stresses that she wants a fast divorce and that she really thinks you can just use a "standard divorce form." You know that your firm has such a form, and you are prepared to look at it.

As you begin to understand that Cameron is really worried about financial matters and wants a sense of closure, you are surprised that Kimberly walks into the room and apologizes for being late to the meeting. Kimberly takes a seat opposite Cameron, and she turns her body away from him. It dawns on you that they are planning for you to represent both of them.

You apologize but tell them that you are worried about conflicts with representing them both, and that you are new to this area of law. They tell you that there is no conflict between them; they both want the divorce. You explain that you are going to have to look into the ethical issues before you can agree to speak with either of them further. They do agree that if you can only represent one of the spouses, you should represent Cameron.

Writing Assignment:

Although you recognize that you need more information before you can give complete advice, you start to "mark up" the relevant tax sections of the firm's standard Divorce Agreement (i.e., delete, edit, or add language) to reflect Cameron's preferred arrangement. You draw attention to your changes by doing them in Track Changes or run a document comparison. You also need to prepare for negotiations and a meeting with the client-matter partner. Write a brief explanation for each of your proposed amendments using the Proposed Revisions to Divorce Agreement form that follows the Divorce Agreement.

Provisions from Firm's Standard Divorce Agreement

ARTICLE VI.—INCOME TAX

1. The parties have heretofore filed joint income tax returns with the appropriate federal and state taxing authorities. Except as otherwise provided herein, all liabilities on any such joint income tax returns shall be equally borne by the parties, and all refunds on such returns shall be equally divided by the parties. The Husband and Wife each hereby warrant and represent to the other that to the best of his or her knowledge all federal, state and local income tax on all joint returns heretofore filed by the parties have been paid, and that no interest or penalty is due with respect thereto, and that no tax deficiency proceeding is pending or threatened thereon.

2. The parties will file [*a joint/separate*] tax return[*s*] for the year 20__.

3. The parties will cooperate with each other in the event that any audit, claim, tax deficiency or other proceeding is brought by the relevant taxing authorities against the parties, or either of them, on account of any joint return heretofore filed. The parties further agree that the costs and expenses of defending such a proceeding shall be equally borne by the parties.

4. [*Husband/Wife*] shall be entitled to the following income tax exemptions, credits and deductions attributable to the [*child/children*] listed above as the [*child/children*] of the parties:

a. The exemption for dependents allowable under Section 151(c) of the U.S. Internal Revenue Code of 1986, as amended (the "Code");

b. The child tax credit allowable under Section 24 of the Code; and

c. [*Description of any other applicable exemptions, credits or deductions.*]

5. If requested by [*husband/wife*], [*wife/husband*] shall promptly sign and deliver to [*husband/wife*] any tax forms required by the Internal Revenue Service or any state taxing authority in order for [*husband/wife*]

to claim the above tax exemptions, credits and deductions relating to the [*child/children*], including but not limited to IRS Form 8332 ("Release/Revocation of Release of Claim to Exemption for Child by Custodial Parent").

Proposed Revision(s) to Divorce Agreement

Privileged and Confidential for Discussion Purposes Only

Section 1:

Section 2:

Section 3:

Section 4:

Section 5:

Points to Consider:

1. What concerns do you have about the couple having filed joint returns and the IRS letter?
2. What recommendations do you have with respect to the children?
3. Can you be the lawyer for both Cameron and Kimberly? What concerns would you have?

Optional Research:

How does your state award child tax credits in divorce?

CHAPTER ELEVEN

EITC

Earning Praise for Your Simplicity

You take your responsibility to the community seriously. Not only is it an obligation that attorneys accept for being licensed, but you believe that you have special skills that should be used to better the world. To that end, you volunteer your time providing legal services. You also work with VITA to prepare tax returns for lower-income taxpayers.

You were recently called by Derek Floyd, a friend of yours who is a manager at the nonprofit Friendly Financial. Friendly Financial engages in outreach to lower-income members of the community. It has begun a new initiative to help members of the community understand tax credits that may be available to them. You find this an exciting opportunity, but you are a bit hesitant because you worry it is beyond your legal expertise.

Derek assures you that Friendly Financial has everything in place to offer financial wellness planning, but it would appreciate if you could create a one-pager focused on the Earned Income Tax Credit to communicate what taxpayers can do to maximize their credit.

While talking to Derek about Friendly Financial's goals for the one-pager, you hear that Friendly Financial is having problems raising money to continue its outreach. Some of their staff is talking about soliciting donors and their year-end strategy.

You try to keep your focus on the goals for the one-pager. The most important thing from Friendly Financial perspective's is that you provide sufficient information so that their clientele understands the credit and understands the risk of abusing the credit. The nonprofit worries that someone will engage in tax evasion, and that this activity will negatively affect both the client and the nonprofit's reputation.

There are three different audiences on which Friendly Financial focuses its efforts:

- Non-native English speakers and recent immigrants
- People who have not completed a high school degree or equivalent
- People who have learning disabilities or other special needs

You are a bit nervous because you are not in the business of marketing, but you are going to try and introduce the tax credit to people who need it. At the same time, you are going to try and counsel people to avoid tax evasion. You recognize that drafting the language will be tricky. People receive a lot of information daily, so you must be succinct and clear in order to best educate the nonprofit's clientele.

There is a lot of public information already available but Friendly Financial thinks something shorter and eye-catch would help those without internet access:

- IRS, Earned Income Tax Credit (EITC), https://www.irs.gov/credits-deductions/individuals/earned-income-tax-credit-eitc
- Center on Budget and Policy Priorities, Learn About Tax Credits, https://www.taxoutreach.org
- Turbo Tax, 5 Facts About the Earned Income Credit, https://turbotax.intuit.com/tax-tips/tax-deductions-and-credits/5-facts-about-the-earned-income-tax-credit/L6YfN8sCL

Writing Assignment:

You agree to undertake one of the one-pagers. You choose the group that you most want to reach and create a draft. You have artistic freedom; therefore, you should decide whether to frame it as a leaflet or as a poster.

Points to Consider:

1. Should you focus more on the amount of the credit or the risks to abusing the credit?
2. Is there any difference for you between representing a pro bono client and a paying client?
3. Can you discuss with wealthy co-workers Friendly Financial's need to raise revenue? Is there a distinction between discussing its need and its strategy?

Optional Research:

The Treasury Inspector General for Tax Administration (TIGTA) is tasked with assessing and reporting on the IRS's compliance with congressionally-imposed reporting requirements for tax credits. Congress was particularly worried about improper payment rates. What does the TIGTA say is IRS's latest payment rates for the EITC?

CHAPTER TWELVE

Tax-Exempts

Asking Nicely Not to Pay Tax

A client at your firm, Arturo Vallese, is a philanthropist in your community. He is particularly fond of dogs and of children. Several years ago he had a golden doodle who saved his toddler from a coyote, and he has contributed to dog-related causes ever since.

Vallese's vision is to create a charity that brings dogs currently being fostered or in shelters to the local high school which serves a lower-income community. Children who volunteer for the program would teach the dogs basic commands. The goal is to improve the lives of both dogs and children. The dogs would benefit from the socialization and their improved chances of adoption. Children would also benefit from working with animals and being entrusted with a responsibility. Studies show this is helpful for all people but particularly for children and particularly for those struggling with trauma.

A partner at your firm, Brittany Chou, had the initial meeting with Vallese. You look over her notes and learn that Vallese has already formed a corporation under the laws of his state to operate the charity. He also has all of the organization's paperwork, operating documents, and employer identification number. Vallese has completed all the necessary financial documentation and will send it for your review. Although Vallese would be thrilled if the program expands beyond his local community, he recognizes that this will be a pilot program that may not spread to other schools. He just really wants to give back to his community.

You get a few more facts from Vallese. The town does have a large ASPCA that places, on average, 1,000 dogs per year. Vallese has no desire for the charity to lobby the local or state governments on behalf of dogs; but, as he thought about it, he thought that some legal changes could really further his mission. You have heard that Vallese likes to go to the state capital and "talk to people" but you do not know about what.

Although Vallese is committed to the project, he would like to be able to raise additional revenue by assuring contributors that they would receive a tax deduction for their donations. You recognize that this means the entity needs to qualify as a § 501(c)(3) public charity.

You know a little bit about the rules but need a quick refresher. You see that the IRS requires for an entity to be a public charity (as opposed to, for example, a private foundation), the entity must:

- be incorporated, an LLC, unincorporated association, or a trust
- have adopted bylaws
- have an employer identification number
- have an active program of fundraising and receive contributions from many sources

Finally, the IRS also requires the entity have a charitable purpose. Section 501(c)(3) provides that entities should be organized and operated exclusively for:

- religious, charitable, scientific, testing for public safety, literary, or educational purposes,
- to foster national or international amateur sports competition (but only if no part of its activities involve the provision of athletic facilities or equipment), or
- for the prevention of cruelty to children or animals

To apply for tax-exempt status, you will need to complete Form 1023 for the entity, one part of which requires:

> **Part IV. Narrative Description of Your Activities.**
> Using an attachment, describe your past, present, and planned activities in a narrative. If you believe that you have already provided some of this information in response

to other parts of this application, you may summarize that information here and refer to the specific parts of the application for supporting details. You may also attach representative copies of newsletters, brochures, or similar documents for supporting details to this narrative. Remember that if this application is approved, it will be open for public inspection. Therefore, your narrative description of activities should be thorough and accurate. Refer to the instructions for information that must be included in your description.

Writing Assignment:

Chou asks you to draft a detailed description of this entities' activities in a way that is both accurate and likely to achieve tax-exempt status. She also tells you that this description needs to be concise, so it is generally best to keep it no more than a couple paragraphs. Reviewing examples of the firm's prior filing, you see that you should include:

- What specific activities are conducted,
- Who participates in the activities,
- Where the entity will conduct the activities,
- When or how often the activities occur,
- What fees, if any, are charged and how the entity determines them, and
- What percentage of the entity's time and resources the entity spends on the activities.

Points to Consider:

1. What additional questions would you like to follow up with Vallese?
2. How certain do you feel that this will qualify as a tax-exempt entity?
3. Do you need to verify material or can you just rely on Chou's notes?

Optional Research:

Except for religious organizations, tax-exempts are required to file Form 990 annually with the IRS to maintain their tax-exempt status. As one example, review the ASCPA's latest filing to see if it engaged in lobbying efforts.

CHAPTER THIRTEEN

Civil Litigation

I Won—and the Government Won

You have rotated into your firm's civil litigation department. Your client, Maxwell Robard, contacted you several weeks ago after being fired from ComputerZ Inc. (ComputerZ). Robard had been ComputerZ's Chief Operating Officer. ComputerZ's CEO and Robard's direct superior was John Amber.

Robard was upset with his former employer. He is 58 years old and, before last year, had always received excellent annual performance reviews. Last year, ComputerZ was acquired by a new company, Bigger is Better (Bigger), in a contentious merger, and ComputerZ is now a subsidiary of Bigger. Bigger's CEO is Brittany Stark, who had assured everyone in the merger that management would be retained, and everyone had been until Robard was fired. Robard was very surprised that his employment was terminated and he was replaced by his 26-year-old second-in-command.

Robard did admit that since the merger work had been difficult for him. He struggled within the new corporate culture. Robard had traditionally worn a suit to work whereas his new colleagues all wore jeans and T-shirts. Robard hung his diplomas on his office walls whereas his new colleagues hung posters of video games. Robard likes to go to the opera and symphony whereas his new colleagues go to the local college's football games and concerts. Nevertheless, Robard continued to meet all of his targets.

His colleagues teased him about his difficulties. They also kept referring to him as "old man" and "senior." Someone left the following note on his desk:

> ComputerZ are not for those who walked with the dinosaurs.

Robard had laughed the comments off, but they had bothered him.

Robard thinks that the problems came to a head at a corporate retreat at another subsidiary of Bigger, TeamBuilding Ex (TBE). During the retreat, there were many team-building and trust-building exercises. Several of them were physically difficult. Not only did they have to do the traditional trust fall, they also had to do what Robard describes as absurd obstacle courses. During one obstacle course, Robard fell and broke his arm. Stark made it very clear to Robard that he was not to blame the broken arm on TBE because it is her passion-project and objected to by several members of the board.

After his fall at TBE, Robard's relationships with his colleagues deteriorated. Many of them questioned his ability to do anything, particularly because of his broken arm. They mockingly carried paperwork for him, all the while telling him he was too old and too fragile for this industry. Robard now wants to sue for wrongful termination. He is not worried about getting a new job. In fact, he already has several interviews lined up. Nevertheless, Robard does not want this to happen to other people in the future. He thinks Bigger is not better. Although he is not really doing this for the money, some compensation would definitely help him as he thinks about an early retirement.

The litigation associate already sent Bigger a demand letter containing a summary of the detrimental conduct and causes of action with a warning that he is unsure of the amount of potential damages. Robard wants to resolve this matter as quickly as possible, so your legal team is preparing for a negotiation with Bigger and its lawyers.

Writing Assignment:

The partner you work for is going to handle most of the negotiations, but you have the task of creating a bullet point list of issues/facts that have important tax consequences. You know you will be judged on how you handle the tax side of the negotiation. Include for the partner a short explanation of why you want to raise a point and why you have placed it where you have in the list.

Name:

Attorney-Client Privileged

Attorneys' Work Product

Preliminary negotiation checklist:

-
-
-
-

Points to Consider:

1. From the tax perspective, should you focus on the physical injury or the age discrimination?
2. Are there issues other than tax that will influence your negotiation?
3. As your fee is structured as a contingent fee on gross damages, do you have to worry about conflicts of interests in any settlement offer?

Optional Research:

Can Robard deduct your fees or will he be taxed on a gross basis?